Samuel Adams

by
Stuart A. Kallen

Visit us at
www.abdopub.com

Published by ABDO Publishing Company, 4940 Viking Drive, Edina, MN 55435. Copyright ©2001 by Abdo Consulting Group, Inc. International copyrights reserved in all countries. No part of this book may be reproduced in any form without written permission from the publisher.

Printed in the United States.

Graphic design: John Hamilton
Cover Design: Maclean Tuminelly

Cover photo: Corbis
Interior photos and illustrations:
    Corbis: p. 6, 9, 11, 15, 17, 23, 35, 36, 43, 45, 47, 49, 51, 52, 55
    John Hamilton: p. 39, 57, 59
    North Wind Picture Archives: p. 5, 13, 18, 19, 21, 25, 27, 29, 30, 33, 40, 41

Library of Congress Cataloging-in-Publication Data

Kallen, Stuart A., 1955-
    Samuel Adams / Stuart Kallen.
        p. cm. — (The founding fathers)
    Includes index.
    Summary: Presents a biography of the Massachusetts radical whose belief in foreceful protest against injustice made him one of the leaders of the American Revolution.
    ISBN 1-57765-008-5
    1. Adams, Samuel, 1722-1803—Juvenile literature.
2. Politicians—United States—Biography—Juvenile literature. 3. United States. Declaration of Independence—Signers—Biography—Juvenile literature. 4. United States—History—Revolution, 1775-1783—Biography—Juvenile Literature. [1. Adams, Samuel, 1722-1803. 2. Politicians. 3. United States—History—Revolution, 1775-1783—Biography.] I. Title.

E302.6.A2 K35 2001
973.3'13'092—dc21
[B]
                                                    98-010969

Contents

Introduction

THE HOOF BEATS OF Paul Revere's horse drummed through the Massachusetts night. From atop his horse Revere yelled a warning: "The British are coming! The British are coming!" As Revere passed farms and villages with his message, people inside their homes loaded their rifles. The bright moonlight revealed two British officers on horseback. Revere turned and rode away at full gallop. He escaped and made his way to Lexington. Later he said, "The heavier British charger... was no match for my lightfooted Yankee horse."

Revere was riding to warn the citizens of Massachusetts. The British army was on the march. It was April 19, 1775, and a war was about to start between the 13 American colonies and Great Britain. America was fighting for its freedom.

Facing page: a portrait of Samuel Adams.

Paul Revere on his famous ride to warn of approaching British soldiers.

Revere reached Lexington. He rode up to the house of Rev. Jonas Clark. Inside, Samuel Adams and John Hancock, leaders in the revolutionary movement, were in hiding. The British were going to arrest the men. Adams had been writing anti-British articles and spreading them throughout the Colonies. Many Americans did not want to separate from Britain. But Adams wanted independence and he wanted it now. If the British caught Adams he would be hung for treason.

Revere approached the house where Adams slept. Eight soldiers guarded the area. The soldiers warned Revere to make no noise lest he disturb the sleeping Adams. "Noise!" cried Revere, "You'll soon have noise enough, the British are coming!"

Within an hour Adams and Hancock were gone. By morning, thundering shots rang out. The town of Lexington would be the site of the first battle of the American Revolutionary War. A war that would drag on for six long, bloody years. For now, however, Adams was happy that the time for independence had come. As he and Hancock prepared to leave Lexington, he turned to his long-time friend and said, "Oh what a glorious morning is this!"

The Boston Politician

THERE WERE TWO branches of the Adams family in Massachusetts in the 1700s. The Adams family who lived in Boston produced Samuel Adams. The Adams family who lived in Braintree (now Quincy, Massachusetts) produced America's second president, John Adams. John was Sam's cousin. Sam, who was born on September 27, 1722, was a leading supporter of the American Revolution. In fact, without Samuel Adams, the revolution might never have happened at all.

Sam's father was Deacon Samuel Adams, a leader in the Puritan church. Deacon Adams owned a malt house that made ingredients for brewing beer.

Samuel Adams, as he looked when he became governor of Massachusetts in 1794.

Young Sam attended Boston Latin School where he studied the Latin language, arithmetic, and reading. When he was only 14 years old, Sam began studying at Harvard College. Sam's father wanted him to join the ministry after college. However, the young man was drawn towards politics.

While Sam was in college, Deacon Adams began a new business. The Deacon and a few friends started a bank. They printed their own money and backed it up with their land and homes. It was called a "land bank" and people in Boston liked the idea.

The British authorities that ruled Massachusetts did not like the land bank. England's governing body, the Parliament, passed a law to shut down Deacon Adams's bank. Since Adams backed the bank with his land, he lost his land and a great deal of money. When the land bank closed, the Adams family became very bitter toward English authorities.

*Samuel Adams went to school at Harvard
University (then Harvard College) at age 14.*

Not Much of a Businessman

WHEN SAMUEL ADAMS graduated from Harvard, he gave a fiery speech. He said that the people of Massachusetts should not have to obey laws passed in England. He thought people in the Colonies should have the right to make their own laws.

After college, Sam went to work in his father's malt house. Tragedy struck in 1748 when the elder Adams died. Samuel inherited his father's business and a large old house on Boston's Purchase Street. But Sam was not a successful businessman. He was always late for appointments. He had trouble with numbers and details. And he wore the same wrinkled brown suit to work day after day.

Adams gave up on the business world and plunged into colonial politics. In 1749, he married Elizabeth Checkley. The couple had five children together, although sadly only two, Samuel and Hannah, lived beyond infancy.

Samuel Adams was not a successful businessman.

Adams the Tax Collector

I N 1756, ADAMS was elected as Boston's tax collector. He was popular with taxpayers because of his easygoing manner. If a taxpayer did not have the money they owed, Adams looked the other way. Hard times fell on Adams in 1757. Elizabeth died, leaving Sam with two small children to raise.

Sam's troubles with his father's land bank continued to drag on. Adams had been printing a newspaper that spoke out against Boston's wealthy families. Massachusetts authorities did not like what Adams wrote. Perhaps this is why they were still demanding money from Sam 15 years after his father's bank closed.

In 1758, authorities decided to sell off Adams's house to pay for the land bank. Sam attended the sale and threatened the sheriff and the would-be buyers. The sheriff ran off, and Adams kept his house. Then he attacked the authorities in his newspaper for harassing honest citizens. Sam's articles were so successful that the authorities backed off. He was able to keep his house.

Samuel Adams was elected as Boston's tax collector in 1756.

Tax Troubles

MEANWHILE, England and France were fighting a war. The war began because the French were setting up forts in Canada and western Pennsylvania. With help from colonial soldiers, the British won the war in 1763. The war, however, left Britain deep in debt.

To pay for the war, the British Parliament began to impose taxes on Americans for the first time. The Parliament thought Americans would be happy to pay for the war. They benefited the most when the French were driven from the Colonies. Plus, Americans were among the wealthiest people in the world. The colonists, however, were furious. They had no representatives in the British Parliament looking out for their interests. Americans all over the Colonies cried out "Taxation without representation is tyranny!"

French and British forces battle during the French and Indian War.

The British ignored the American complaints and passed the Stamp Act of 1765. The act put a tax on all printed material. This included legal documents, newspapers, and even playing cards.

In the summer of 1765, Adams decided to show his outrage over the Stamp Act. He joined a secret club called the Sons of Liberty. This Boston club met to figure out ways to stop the Stamp Act. Before long, the Sons of Liberty would be making history.

An example of a British stamp imposed as a tax on Americans.

Samuel Adams speaks out against the British at a meeting of the Sons of Liberty.

Burnings and Riots

ANDREW OLIVER had just been appointed stamp master of Massachusetts. He was to oversee the collection of the stamp tax. On August 14, acting under orders from Adams, the Sons of Liberty hung an effigy of Oliver in a tree. (An effigy is a stuffed dummy meant to symbolize a living person.)

When the sheriff tried to remove the effigy, the Sons of Liberty threatened to kill him. That evening, a large mob paraded around Oliver's house. They burned down a new building that was to house the stamp tax office. Then they threw rocks through Oliver's windows and broke into his house looking for him. Oliver escaped. The next day he resigned from his office.

Facing page: a tax official hung in effigy.

Glorious News.

BOSTON, Friday 11 o'Clock, 16th *May* 1766.
THIS Inftant arrived here the Brig Harrifon, belonging
to *John Hancock*, Efq; Captain *Shubael Coffin*, in 6
Weeks and 2 Days from LONDON, with important
News, as follows.

From the LONDON GAZETTE.

Weftminfter, March 18th, 1766.

THIS day his Majefty came to the Houfe of Peers, and being in his royal
robes feated on the throne with the ufual folemnity, Sir Francis Moli-
neux, Gentleman Ufher of the Black Rod, was fent with a Meffage
from his Majefty to the Houfe of Commons, commanding their atten-
dance in the Houfe of Peers. The Commons being come thither accordingly,
his Majefty was pleafed to give his royal affent to

An ACT to REPEAL an Act made in the laft Seffion of Parliament, in-
tituled, an Act for granting and applying certain Stamp-Duties and other Duties
in the Britifh Colonies and Plantations in America, towards further defraying
the expences of defending, protecting and fecuring the fame, and for amending
fuch parts of the feveral Acts of Parliament relating to the trade and revenues
of the faid Colonies and Plantations, as direct the manner of determining and
recovering the penalties and forfeitures therein mentioned.

Alfo ten public bills, and feventeen private ones.

Yefterday there was a meeting of the principal Merchants concerned in the
American trade, at the King's Arms tavern in Cornhill, to confider of an Ad-
drefs to his Majefty on the beneficial Repeal of the late Stamp-Act.

Yefterday morning about eleven o'clock a great number of North-American
Merchants went in their coaches from the King's Arms tavern in Cornhill to the
Houfe of Peers, to pay their duty to his Majefty, and to exprefs their fatisfac-
tion at his figning the Bill for Repealing the American Stamp-Act, there was
upwards of fifty coaches in the proceffion.

Laft night the faid gentleman difpatched an exprefs for Falmouth, with fif-
teen copies of the Act for repealing the Stamp-Act, to be forwarded immediately for New York.

Orders are given for feveral merchantmen in the river to proceed to fea immediately on their refpective voyages to North America, fome of whom have
been cleared out fince the firft of November laft.

Yefterday meffengers were difpatched to Birmingham, Sheffield, Manchefter,
and all the great manufacturing towns in England, with an account of the final
decifion of an auguft affembly relating to the Stamp-Act.

When the KING went to the Houfe of Peers to give the Royal Affent, there
was fuch a vaft Concourfe of People, huzzaing, clapping Hands, &c. that it
was feveral Hours before His Majefty reached the Houfe.

Immediately on His Majefty's Signing the Royal Affent to the Repeal of the
Stamp-Act the Merchants trading to America difpatched a Veffel which had been
in waiting, to put into the firft Port on the Continent with the Account.

There were the greateft Rejoicings poffible in the City of London, by all Ranks
of People, on the TOTAL Repeal of the Stamp-Act.—the Ships in the River
difplayed all their Colours, Illuminations and Bonfires in many Parts. — In
fhort, the Rejoicings were as great as was ever known on any Occafion.

It is faid the Acts of Trade relating to America would be taken under Con-
fideration, and all Grievances removed. The Friends to America are very pow-
erful, and difpofed to affift us to the utmoft of their Ability.

Capt. Blake failed the fame Day with Capt. Coffin, and Capt. Sha and a Fort-
night before him, both bound to this Port.

*It is impoffible to exprefs the Joy the Town it now in, on receiving the
above, great, glorious and important NEWS—The Bells in all the Churches
were immediately fet a Ringing, and we hear the Day for a general Rejoicing
will be the beginning of next Week.*

PRINTED for the Benefit of the PUBLIC, by
Drapers, Edes & Gill, Green & Ruffell, and *Fleets.*
The Cuftomers to the Bofton Papers may have the above gratis at their refpective
Offices.

[Fac-fimile of an original in the library of the Mafs. Hift. Society. — ED.]

Later in the month, furious colonists attacked the homes of customs officials. Then they went on to sack and burn the house of Lieutenant Governor Thomas Hutchinson. By the time the fires were put out, the Stamp Act was also finished. England repealed the tax the next year.

Above: a Stamp Act riot in the streets of Boston. Facing page: a 1766 handbill announcing the repeal of the British Stamp Act.

More Taxes and Troubles

ADAMS'S STAND against the tax made him popular enough to run for political office. He was elected to the Massachusetts House of Representatives in 1765. Within two weeks of taking his seat in the House, Adams was appointed to several important committees. But he knew the troubles with England were not over. Adams warned, "This is not the end. There will be more bad laws. We must be prepared."

Adams's dire predictions proved true. After Parliament repealed the Stamp Act, they passed a group of new taxes. The Townsend Acts of 1767 levied taxes on glass, paint, paper, and tea brought in from Britain.

The tax on tea was only a few pennies, but it enraged Americans. Every time they had a cup of tea, people were reminded that the British controlled them. Adams and the Sons of Liberty urged people to boycott (stop buying) British tea.

The true Sons of Liberty

And Supporters of the Non-Importation

Agreement,

ARE determined to rëfent any the leaft Infult or Menace offer'd to any one or more of the feveral Committees appointed by the Body at Faneuil-Hall, and chaftife any one or more of them as they deferve ; and will alfo fupport the Printers in any Thing the Committees fhall defire them to print.

☞ AS a Warning to any one that fhall affront as aforefaid, upon fure Information given, one of thefe Advertifements will be pofted up at the Door or Dwelling-Houfe of the Offender.

A handbill printed by the Sons of Liberty
supporting a boycott of British goods.

When the boycott began, women gave "non-tea" parties where they served milk and juice. Coffee quickly became a popular drink. Some folks drank tea made from wild flowers and herbs. The boycott was partially successful, but many Americans still drank English tea.

The tea tax, however, stirred up American anger. The British felt they had to do something to keep the peace. On October 1, 1768, 4,000 British soldiers landed in Boston. Their uniforms included red wool coats, so people called them "redcoats." The British troops found a peaceful town, but behind closed doors Adams and others were talking about armed resistance.

As a politician, Adams listened to the problems of Boston's farmers, workers, and common citizens. During town meetings at the city's Faneuil Hall, Adams argued that colonists should reject taxes levied by the British Parliament. He demanded that Americans be given the same rights as British citizens. And he used a word that could have landed him in jail for treason — "independence."

Facing page: a patriotic woman spinning cloth to avoid importing British fabric.

The Boston Massacre

T HE REDCOATS camped on Boston Commons. All day long they marched and drilled to the music of fifes and drums. Soon, Parliament repealed all the taxes in the Townsend Acts—except the tax on tea. For several years an uneasy peace existed in Boston between the redcoats and the Sons of Liberty.

The redcoats were a rough bunch—tough soldiers with little to do. They were itching for a fight. On March 2, 1770, they got their chance. A rope-maker named Nicholas Ferrier exchanged insults with a redcoat. Soon, several men on both sides started to brawl.

Facing page: British troops fire on an angry mob during the Boston Massacre.

Several days later a crowd gathered. The Bostonians began pelting the redcoats with snowballs and sticks. Young boys called them lobsterbacks. Someone yelled "Fire!" and the redcoats shot their muskets into the crowd. When the smoke cleared, five Americans lay dead.

Samuel Adams called the incident the "Boston Massacre." The soldiers were put on trial, but they were found innocent for reasons of self-defense. Sam Adams was outraged.

Things quieted down after the Boston Massacre, but the lamp burned bright night after night in Adams's window as he tried to keep the patriotic cause alive. Between 1770 and 1772, Adams wrote more than 40 anti-British articles for the *Boston Gazette*.

Facing page: Samuel Adams demanding that British troops withdraw after the Boston Massacre.

Committees of Correspondence

I N THE AUTUMN of 1772, Adams started a group with his supporters called the Committees of Correspondence. The committees were to be a letter-writing group. Their purpose was to keep rural villages up-to-date on their rights as American citizens.

The committees may have started out telling people about their rights, but Adams soon changed the focus. He began sending out strong anti-British messages. Before long, 80 committees were formed in Massachusetts. The practice soon spread to the other colonies. Some were as far away as South Carolina.

Facing page: Samuel Adams started the Committees of Correspondence in 1772.

More Tea Troubles

THE TEA TAX continued to strike a nerve with Americans. They didn't like Britain's King George III controlling their lives from 3,000 miles (4,828 km) away. The British made things even worse when they granted the British East India Company sole rights to sell tea in the Colonies. Americans did not like one company controlling all the tea they drank. Angry colonists demanded action.

From across the Atlantic Ocean, the British East India Company had no idea that Americans were outraged. The company sent a fleet of ships loaded with tea to American ports in 1773. Three of those ships were to sail to Boston Harbor.

Facing page: England's King George III.

When the ships were spotted off the coast, the Committees of Correspondence began their work. Leaders decided they would not allow the tea to be brought ashore. In Philadelphia and New York, the tea was not unloaded. The ships, full of tea, sailed back to England. All eyes turned to Boston to see what would happen with the tea troubles there.

Massachusetts Governor Thomas Hutchinson was determined that the tea *would* be unloaded. Hutchinson wanted to see the tea tax collected, but he had other motives. His two sons worked for the British East India Company. They would make a huge profit when the tea was sold in Boston.

On November 11, 1773, the first of the tea ships dropped anchor outside of Boston. During the next three weeks, two more ships arrived. The ships were tied up at the wharf, but dockworkers refused to unload them. British warships sailed into view with their cannons pointed at the Boston dock. Tensions began to mount.

Facing page: the Beaver II, *a replica of the* Beaver, *one of three ships boarded by angry colonists during the Boston Tea Party.*

The Boston Tea Party

HUTCHINSON ISSUED a deadline. He said all taxes on the tea aboard the ships must be paid by December 16. If the taxes were not paid, the governor would order the army to unload the tea. December 16 arrived cold and rainy, but the weather did not keep 7,000 people from gathering at the Old South Meeting House. They were there to attend a meeting organized by Sam Adams.

The gathering was the largest group of people ever assembled in Boston at the time. People spilled out of the church onto the streets. Speakers got up to demand the ships return to England with the tea. Adams got up and motioned the cheering crowd to silence. He said, "This meeting can do nothing more to save the country." The crowd started yelling "To the wharf! Tonight Boston Harbor is a teapot!"

Facing page: Boston's Old South Meeting House.

Above: Boston citizens disguised as Mohawk Indians seize British tea.

Facing page: boxes of tea are tossed into Boston Harbor.

Fifty men came out of a back room in the church. They were wrapped in blankets, they had their faces painted like Mohawk Indians, and they carried axes. The crowd recognized the men as Boston's most prominent citizens. The men, however, hoped their disguises would confuse the British spies that were in the crowd.

The crowd surged down to the docks. The men disguised as Indians split into three groups, one for each tea ship. They boarded the ships quietly so they would not arouse the British navy. The ships were crammed full of chests of tea, each one weighing 320 pounds (145 kg). The men hauled the cargo onto the deck, broke open the chests, and dumped the tea over the sides of the ships. Before long all 342 chests of tea were dumped into Boston Harbor.

The First Continental Congress

T HE BOSTON TEA PARTY, organized by Samuel Adams, enraged the British government. They reacted by passing a series of laws to punish the colonists. One law would force the Bostonians to pay for all the tea they ruined. Another would force them to house and feed British soldiers in their homes. In April 1774, a military commander, General Thomas Gage, replaced Governor Hutchinson. Gage closed Boston Harbor to all ships in order to starve the people into good behavior.

On September 5, 1774, Samuel Adams and 47 delegates met at Carpenters' Hall in Philadelphia. The meeting was called the First Continental

Congress. The Colonies wanted to resist the British but could not agree on what should be done. The Southern delegates wanted to bargain with the British. Samuel Adams wanted to declare total independence.

When the meeting broke up on October 28, the group had a list of demands they sent to King George. The Continental Congress wanted civil rights in the Colonies. They created a group of representatives from each colony to tighten the ban on English goods.

Patrick Henry speaking at the First Continental Congress. Samuel Adams wanted to declare total independence from England

"Liberty or Death!"

T HE BRITISH crackdown became known as the "Intolerable Acts." To fight back, militia groups called the "minutemen" were organized. The name meant they would be ready to fight at a moment's notice. Every town square in Massachusetts soon became a drilling ground for groups of minutemen.

On March 23, 1775, Patrick Henry made his famous speech, "The war is inevitable and let it come! I know not what course the others may take, but as for me, give me liberty or give me death!"

On April 18, 1775, Americans found out that the redcoats were planning to march on Concord, 20 miles (32 km) from Boston. The redcoats' orders were to find gunpowder that was hidden by the minutemen, and they were to arrest Sam

---

Patrick Henry giving his famous "Give me liberty, or give me death" speech.

Adams and his friend John Hancock. Paul Revere mounted his horse and rode through the Massachusetts night yelling, "The British are coming! The British are coming!"

On the morning of April 19, about 500 British soldiers left Boston for Concord. Adams and Hancock were in nearby Lexington. Thanks to Paul Revere's warning, the two revolutionaries avoided capture.

Minutemen started to beat a drumroll at dawn to call the soldiers into action. The American Revolution had begun.

Lexington and Concord

WHEN THE REDCOATS came to Lexington, they saw 70 Americans with their rifles primed. The British fired on the colonists, killing eight men and wounding 10. The frightened minutemen ran from the battlefield. Later in the morning, the British marched into Concord. There, they were met by 1,500 armed men. Some were minutemen. Some were regular citizens inflamed by the morning's massacre in Lexington. A battle ensued, leaving many dead on both sides.

The minutemen scattered. The British marched back to Lexington. As the redcoats traveled down the road, minutemen shot at them from behind trees and rocks. Trapped in a hail of gunfire, the British panicked. By the time the redcoats ran back to Boston, they had lost 273 men. The Americans lost 93.

Minutemen battle British forces at the Battle of Lexington.

The Second Continental Congress

REPRESENTATIVES from America's 13 colonies called a meeting in Philadelphia. On May 10, 1775, the Second Continental Congress met to organize resistance to the British. Three of the Massachusetts delegates sent to the congress were John Adams, Samuel Adams, and John Hancock.

John Adams had written a plan for the congress in his diary. He thought the program for the Continental Congress was to "inform Great Britain very frankly that hitherto we were free... [and] we ought immediately to adopt... a Continental Army, to appoint a General... and take upon ourselves the pay, clothing, armor, and munitions of the troops."

Many of John Adams's radical ideas were too extreme for a lot of the Southern delegates. The sessions droned on through a hot, humid summer as the delegates argued over what to do. In June, John and Sam nominated George Washington as commander-in-chief of the Continental Army. In this nomination, the other delegates agreed.

A portrait of John Adams.

The Bloody Battles of Boston

W HILE THE ADAMS cousins were debating in Philadelphia, armies were on the move. Seven thousand American soldiers surrounded Boston in a circle 16 miles (25 km) long. Four thousand British troops remained in the city.

On June 16, 1775, 1,200 Americans moved to fortify Breed's Hill on the Charlestown peninsula. British warships fired cannonballs at them from the sea. When 2,200 redcoats marched off the ships, Americans opened fire on them from their houses. Wave after wave of redcoats marched on, suffering in the heat and under the weight of their 120-pound (54-kg) packs. Within an hour, 1,054 redcoats were shot; 226 of them died. The Americans lost 140 men.

Facing page: the Battle of Breed's Hill (Bunker Hill).

George Washington, commander-in-chief of the Continental Army.

After the battle, Washington took command of the American Army. Within a few weeks, thousands more soldiers arrived from Pennsylvania, Maryland, and Virginia. The men, however, were so short on ammunition that each man was only allowed nine cartridges. The men wore tattered clothes and had no overcoats for cold weather. Some even had to fight in bare feet. This problem was soon solved by patriotic American women who went to work sewing coats and uniforms for the men. As was common in those days, sickness and disease killed more soldiers than guns and cannons.

General Washington was highly respected by the British. They could not understand why he was taking part in an illegal revolution with "riff raff like Sam Adams."

Americans Win Their Freedom

O
N JULY 4, 1776, the Continental Congress issued the Declaration of Independence. The first signer was John Hancock, who wrote his name in a huge script. Hancock wanted to make sure King George III could read it without his spectacles. The document was written by Thomas Jefferson and declared the United States officially free of British rule.

The war raged on for five more years. The ill-fed and ill-equipped Continental Army won a few battles, but they lost even more to the redcoats. Several long, cold winters left the American soldiers cold, sick, and dying at military camps. Sam Adams did not like the way Washington was running the army. He fought to have Washington removed as commander. When his attempts failed, Adams's good standing with the other patriots was ruined.

In the end, the Americans finally beat the redcoats at Yorktown, Virginia, on October 17, 1781. The British surrender at Yorktown was the end of British rule in the colonies. Benjamin Franklin, John Adams, and John Jay met the British in Paris to sign a peace treaty.

The Declaration of Independence.

After the Revolution

S AMUEL ADAMS was a very effective radical leader. He was able to move crowds to action while he worked behind the scenes. Tearing down a government, however, was easier than setting up a new one. Many did not think Samuel Adams was up to the task. One French minister wrote about Adams, "a man whose resolute character was so useful to the Revolution at its origin, but who shows himself so ill suited to the conduct of affairs in an organized government."

Facing page: a statue of Samuel Adams stands in front of Boston's Faneuil Hall, the site where Adams and other patriots often spoke at town meetings, rallying against British oppression.

SAMUEL ADAMS
1722—1803
A PATRIOT
HE ORGANIZED THE REVOLUTION

When he signed the Declaration of Independence, Adams was at the height of his career. But with independence, America no longer needed an agitator (a man to whip the emotions of a mob). His most important work had been done between 1765 and 1776.

Samuel Adams did not give up on politics. He served as lieutenant governor of Massachusetts. In 1794, Adams became governor of that state. Adams retired from public life in 1797. He was at last a wealthy man thanks to some sound real estate investments. Adams would sit on the doorstep or wander around his garden talking with friends about old times. When his friend Thomas Jefferson was elected president in 1800, Adams wrote him, "The Storm is over, and we are in port."

As Adams aged, he suffered from nerve disorders. On October 2, 1803, the 81-year-old patriot died. Boston's bells tolled for 30 minutes in mourning. Flags flew at half-mast, and thousands turned out to pay respects to Samuel Adams. The Congress of the United States voted to wear black armbands for one year in memory of the man who led America in achieving independence.

Samuel Adams wasn't the greatest politician or businessman. But his stirring words and his ability to move people to action made him a hero of the Revolution. Without the words, writing, and deeds of Samuel Adams, America might never have won its freedom.

The grave of Samuel Adams, at Boston's Granary Burying Ground.

Timeline

Sept. 27, 1722 .. Samuel Adams born in Boston, Massachusetts.

1736 .... Enters Harvard College in Boston.

1749 .... Marries Elizabeth Checkley. The couple would have five children together.

1756 .... Elected tax collector for Boston.

1757 .... His wife, Elizabeth, dies.

1764 .... Marries Elizabeth Wells.

1765 .... Joins a secret club called the Sons of Liberty. Elected to the Massachusetts House of Representatives.

1772 .... Starts a group with his supporters called the Committees of Correspondence.

1773 .... Helps organize the Boston Tea Party.

1774 .... Delegate to the First Continental Congress.

1775 .... Delegate to the Second Continental Congress.

1776 .... Signs the Declaration of Independence.

1789 .... Appointed Lieutenant Governor of Massachusetts.

1794 .... Becomes Governor of Massachusetts.

Oct. 2, 1803 ..... Dies in Boston at the age of 81 years.

Where on the Web?

The American Revolution Home Page
http://webpages.homestead.com/revwar/files/
ADAMS2.HTM

The American Sons of Liberty
http://americansonsofliberty.com/samadams.htm

Rebels With a Vision
http://www.rebelswithavision.com/
SamuelAdams.net/

U.S. History's Signers of the Declaration of
Independence
http://www.ushistory.org/declaration/signers/
adams_s.htm

Colonial Hall's A Look at America's Founders
http://www.colonialhall.com/adamss/adamss.asp

Glossary

American Revolution: the war between Great Britain and its American Colonies that lasted from 1775 to 1783. America won its independence in the war.

boycott: to try to change the actions of a company or government by refusing to buy their products.

The Colonies: the British territories that made up the first 13 states of the United States. The 13 colonies included New Hampshire, Massachusetts, Rhode Island, Connecticut, New York, New Jersey, Pennsylvania, Delaware, Maryland, Virginia, North Carolina, South Carolina, and Georgia.

Constitution: the document that spells out the principles and laws governing the United States.

Constitutional Convention: the meeting of men who wrote the United States Constitution.

Continental Army: the army that fought the British in the Revolutionary War.

Continental Congress: lawmakers who governed the 13 Colonies after they declared their independence from Great Britain.

debate: to discuss an issue in order to reach the best solution.

Declaration of Independence: the document written by Thomas Jefferson that declared America's independence from Great Britain.

effigy: a stuffed dummy meant to symbolize a living person.

Federalist: a political party that favors a strong central government over the states.

House of Representatives: a governing body elected by popular vote to rule a nation.

militia: a group of citizens enrolled in military service during a time of emergency.

Index